PUTTER PERFECTION

THE GROUNDBREAKING GUIDE TO FINDING THE RIGHT FIT FOR YOUR GAME

Richard Lane
P.O. Box 672
Atlanta, IL 61723

SEAN WEIR

Published by Overspin Media

Cover and book design by Adina Cucicov at Flamingo Designs
Photos and web site by Jon Berezay
Logos by Carrie Gaertig Design
Illustrations generously provided by Never Compromise

ISBN: 978-0-615-49260-5

CONTENTS

INTRODUCTION

I once spoke with a chef who is also a restaurant design consultant. One thing he said really stuck with me: "You need to look at the menu first and then design the kitchen around it."

In other words, if you don't consider your ingredients first, you risk purchasing the wrong equipment.

The same could be said for putters and putting, because if you purchase a putter without regard to your own personal ingredients—your physique, putting approach and other individual attributes—you are creating a recipe for trouble.

Yet that's exactly what most recreational golfers do. They buy a putter right off the retail rack and try to make it work. They fit their strokes to their putters, rather than the other way around. In other words, they set themselves up for failure without even knowing it.

But by picking up this book, you have decided that you no longer want to fly blind on the putting green. You want to understand your putter better. You want to know how your putter works, so that you will know how to begin the process of finding the right fit for you and your game. In other words, you want to achieve what I call *putter perfection.*

As leading instructor Dave Pelz once told me, "There's not *one* putter for all golfers, but there is a *best* putter for every single golfer."

❧ ❧ ❧

The putter accounts for approximately 40 percent of the strokes in an average round of golf. Simply put, if you're serious about improving your game, you really need to know how your putter works.

Personal club fitting is the new frontier of golf improvement. Gone are the days of just grabbing the prettiest putter and hoping for the best. Ignorance is not bliss when it comes to putters. If you want to raise your game, you need to understand how you can harness basic putter fitting fundamentals to your advantage—just as the tour professionals do.

So what, exactly, is putter fitting? It's simply the act of matching your equipment to you and your game. Pick up your putter. How long is it? What does it weigh? What is the angle between the shaft and the sole? When you balance the shaft on a finger, does the toe of the putter dip toward the ground, or does the face of the putter remain parallel to the sky?

The fundamentals of putter fitting are found in the answers to these questions. When you understand and apply these fundamentals, you can fit your putter to your physique and your stroke. In other words, you can get your putter working for you, instead of against you.

I should mention that if you are looking for some magic cure for your putting woes, then this isn't the book for you. This is not an instructional book (and even if it was, there is probably no magic cure for your putting woes!).

Rather, this is a book about how your putter works. It is a book about the fundamentals of putter fitting, and how the proper fit can maximize your potential and shave strokes off your score.

ⵊ ⵊ ⵊ

So who am I to write this book? Well, let me start by saying that I am not an elite golfer or instructor. In fact, I am just like most of you reading this book. I'm an average recreational golfer with a job and a family. I struggle to find the time to golf as much as I would like. And yes, I experience my share of struggles on the green.

What's different about me is that I have made it my vocation to learn as much as possible about putters, and to share my knowledge with others so that they, like me, might use it to help improve their performance.

But you don't have to be a putter nut to benefit from learning more about your putter and how it works. By simply opening this book, you have taken a major step toward improving the fit of your putter—and, by extension, your putting performance.

Before we begin, I want to emphasize an important point: Your personal putting approach is crucial to the fitting equation.

For example, some instructors believe that it is best to putt from a crouched setup, with the eyes directly over the ball and target line. Others, however, recommend a more upright setup, with the eyes slightly inside the target line instead of directly over the ball. Naturally, these different setup approaches will necessitate different putter lengths.

Another example: Some instructors teach a "straight-back, straight-through" style of putting stroke, while others are proponents of the arcing stoke. The rub is that the type of stroke you employ may change the type of putter balance that's best for your game.

Do you see where this is headed? *Different putting approaches naturally yield different fitting recommendations.*

Otherwise, putter fitting would simply be a universal mathematical formula based on your height, arm length and hand size. But in practice, putter fitting is philosophical as well as mathematical. Your own individual optical and physical quirks will also play a role in finding the right fit.

🌾 🌾 🌾

So what's the best fit for you? That's a trick question, because if you've been paying attention, you already know that there's no easy answer.

In order to make the most of this book, you will need to do your homework. You will have to confirm or investigate the putting approach that best works for you. Ideally, this will be done with the input of a trusted instructor, either in person or through published works.

Again, the mission of this book isn't to tell you how to putt. The mission is to *empower* you with the knowledge needed to understand how your putter works. Along the way, you will find answers to your fitting questions, or at least learn the right questions to ask. You may even be able to immediately diagnose nagging putting problems that could be related to your putter.

The Archer—or The Arrow?

Some folks are dismissive of putter fitting, particularly when it comes to the average golfer. They like to say that "it's the archer, not the arrow." In other words, if your aim is off or your mechanics are poor, it doesn't matter what you've got in your hands.

To some degree, that is true. Equipment alone will not cure poor putting mechanics. But does that mean that putter fitting is just hocus-pocus? Does that mean that putter fitting is useful only for elite players, such as those on the PGA and LPGA tours? Does that mean that the struggling golfer should just continue to use an ill-fitting putter?

Of course not. An ill-fitting putter never helps. Golfers of all skill levels will benefit from using a putter that fits as opposed to one that doesn't.

I should add that this book does not intend to diminish or dismiss the importance of clubfitting professionals. A formal fitting can work wonders, as can a good putting lesson.

But the fact is that many of us struggle to find the time or resources for receiving personal attention. Therefore, this book is designed to help you be your own informed advocate when shopping for a putter or evaluating your current putter. It will also help you better understand your options if and when you do seek the input of a clubfitting professional.

On that note, it's important to know that there's an exception to every rule, and the same goes for some of the basic "rules" discussed in this book. You might ultimately end up rejecting some of these rules. But as a wise man once said, it's best to know the rules before you break them.

You are about to embark on an exciting journey of discovery. In fact, you will soon know more than the average golf retail clerk when it comes to the subject of putter fitting, and you will be empowered to make savvier decisions when purchasing or modifying a putter.

In other words, you *will* find the right putter for you, and you *will* raise your game. On that note, let's roll.

Sean Weir
Founder & Editor
PutterZone.com
sean@putterzone.com

1

"THE MAGIC IS IN THE FITTING"

You might say that the modern putter was born in 1959, amid the dim light of a humble garage in Redwood City, California.

It was then and there that Karsten Solheim crafted his first putter, the 1A blade, and his concepts would soon ignite a revolution in putter design.

At the time, Solheim worked for General Electric. It wasn't until 1966 that he resigned from GE to start Karsten Manufacturing, the parent company of his PING brand, so named for the "ping" sound of the putter upon contact. A year later, Julius Boros won the Phoenix Open with what would become known as Solheim's masterwork—the PING Anser model putter.

According to lore, Solheim initially sketched his "answer" on the sleeve of a vinyl record album in 1966. The putter featured a cavity-back design with heel-toe weighting, as well as a distinctive "plumber's neck" offset hosel. At the suggestion of his wife, he removed the 'w' from "answer" so it would better fit on the club.

The Anser blew the doors open to a new era in putters, one in which performance-oriented design and unbridled innovation would leave the simple blades of yesteryear in the dust. The Anser has since become the world's most iconic and copied putter, and "Anser-style" putters remain dominant on the professional circuits.

There have since been other enduring flashpoints in the evolution of the modern putter, such as the bestselling 2-Ball putter by Odyssey Golf.

But it's really over the past five years or so that the era of the modern putter has really hit its stride with a dizzying, and sometimes disorienting, array of shapes, styles and technologies.

Putter brands are proliferating, from the recent groundswell of artisan designers to major golf equipment companies getting into the putter business for the first time. And a single brand might offer a dozen different models within one line of putters, ranging from traditional shapes to putters that look like UFOs.

You now have putters with adjustable weights, interchangeable faces and swappable alignment cues. Face inserts range from aluminum to polymer, and a variety of face groove technologies aim to offer a better roll. Stock putter weights are increasingly varied, and you even have the Heavy Putter, which can weigh up to 500 grams more than a traditional putter.

Companies also routinely roll out technologies that are supposedly the next "big thing" in putters—only to abandon them a year later in favor of new designs and concepts!

Who knows what the future holds. Will there be another revolutionary moment in putter design? Or will it be more evolutionary? Is there a next big thing really out there somewhere, or is it now a tinkerer's game?

It's hard to say. But we can't wait for the future. We have to make sense of the putter options that are available to us right now, and to seek the right fit.

As Mike Clinton of GolfTEC said, "The equipment is close to maxing out to the legal limits. So where can the player find an advantage? It's in figuring out the right club setup out of hundreds of possibilities. The magic is in the fitting."

He wasn't speaking specifically about putters, but it rings true whether you are talking about drivers or irons or, yes, putters. The magic is, indeed, in the fitting.

🌿 🌿 🌿

You are now ready to tap into this magic. In the following chapters, you will learn the essential fundamentals of putter fitting, and how they can be harnessed to raise your game. These fundamentals include:

Length

The proper putter length will help you achieve your optimal setup for a more fluid and repeatable stroke.

Lie Angle

The proper lie angle will give you a better chance of keeping the ball on line, and will help you avoid mystifying misses.

Loft

The proper loft will help the ball achieve true roll more quickly, minimizing bouncing and skidding for enhanced accuracy and distance control.

Balance

Matching the balance of a putter to your personal stroke will foster a smoother, more reliable path from takeaway through impact.

Alignment

Finding a putter that can visually confirm and conform to your target line will ensure consistent accuracy.

Weight

The right swingweight for your physique and mechanics will enable you to strike a beneficial balance of touch, comfort and distance control.

Feel

Using a putter that offers rewarding sensations will inspire you to practice more, and can help you gain valuable feedback.

Grip

The right grip for your hands will breed comfort and confidence, and will help you make a consistent stroke.

There you have it—the fundamentals of putter fitting in a nutshell. But before we delve into them more deeply, we are going to tee off with a brief look at the different types of putters.

2

TYPES OF PUTTERS

Prior to Karsten Solheim's Anser, the most common putter style was the classic blade. Sure, you might see the occasional mallet-style head, but for the first half of the 20th century, the words "putter" and "innovation" were rarely uttered in the same sentence.

By the 1980s, however, the putter industry began to really break the mold. A breakthrough moment occurred in 1986 when Jack Nicklaus, in the twilight of his career, won the Masters while wielding an oversized aluminum MacGregor Response ZT putter.

Prior to the tournament, sales of the Response ZT were negligible. But after the Masters, MacGregor "couldn't make enough."

According to lore, when McGregor's putter designer Clay Long first showed Nicklaus the Response ZT, Nicklaus asked, "Is this a joke?"

This tells you everything you need to know about the evolution and innovation of the putter over the past 25 years. Indeed, by today's standards, the Response ZT looks relatively tame and conventional. Putters now come in so many shapes and sizes that they almost resist categorization.

But at the risk of over-generalizing, the following three categories will help you become more comfortable with the vast array of choices and help you focus on investigating putter types that fit your game.

Classic blades

These are what you see when you watch old footage of Arnold Palmer and his Wilson 8802 putter. Classic blades are thin and lean, with the shaft mounted at the heel. Classic blades are not very forgiving. For reasons explained later in this book, they typically appeal to golfers with a pronounced arcing stroke.

Modern blades

Karsten Solheim ushered in the era of the modern blade with the Anser putter. Modern blades are typically "perimeter weighted," which makes them more forgiving than classic blades. Modern blades come in various shapes and sizes, to the point where the line between mallet and blade is increasingly fuzzy.

Mallets

The term "mallet" is also very general, encompassing the wide variety of putters that have more overall girth than blades. You will also find an assortment of radical shapes in the mallet category. If it looks like a spaceship, it's probably a mallet. The term "mid mallet" is often used to describe a smaller mallet.

🌱 🌱 🌱

Generally speaking, mallets are viewed as more forgiving, particularly when compared to classic blades. Among golfers, you have "blade people" and "mallet people," and those who don't care one way or the other as long as it helps the ball reach the hole.

As explained in the following chapters, the type of putter you play can have a significant impact on a proper fit and resulting performance. The good news is that there is enough variation and innovation in the putter market today that you can find modern blades with many of the qualities typically associated with mallets, and vice versa. This gives you the luxury of being a "blade" or "mallet" person without ignoring the fitting factors that are right for you.

LENGTH

At your local sporting goods store or golf retailer, you will find that nearly all of the putters on the floor are either 34 or 35 inches long. Consequently, that's what most people buy, and they don't give it much thought once they leave the store. It's a recipe for trouble, because if your putter length doesn't fit your physique and setup, you will make detrimental compensations in your setup and stroke.

Think about it. Golfers come in all shapes, sizes and heights, right? Yet two lengths of putters are supposed to essentially fit all of them? Absurd.

On the professional tours, you see a much wider variety putter lengths, all fit for the individual golfer, right down to the half or quarter inch, and sometimes to an eighth of an inch. Why? Because the professionals can't afford to be careless about their putter length. There is just too much money at stake.

But even if you're not playing for the big bucks, you would be wise to consider the following fact, despite the paltry options at your local golf retailer: *There is no "standard" putter length.*

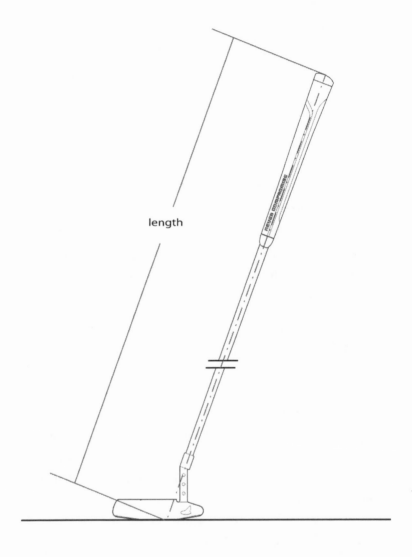

length

Questionable Standards

Let's review how 35 inches became the "standard" putter length for men. According to lore, back when golfers bought their gear at local pro shops instead of superstores, the putters and other clubs were placed in golf bags at the point of purchase. A length of 35 inches allowed the putter to stick out of the bag, and thus a "standard" was born.

In other words, the primary consideration wasn't performance, but rather merchandising.

To be fair, anecdotal accounts from the PGA Tour suggest that the 34- to 35-inch range still fits the widest bandwidth of professional male players. But again, those players are typically fit to the half or quarter inch, and examples abound of professionals using putters that fall well outside of the 34- to 35-inch range.

Still, the major equipment companies and retailers have little incentive to challenge the so-called standards. After all, manufacturers need to control costs, and retailers want to avoid inventory nightmares. In that context, it's unrealistic to expect them to make and merchandise six or eight lengths of every putter model right down to the half inch. So even with the advent of online shopping and drop-shipping, many putters are still only offered in two or three stock lengths.

The limitations in available stock putter lengths can have a psychological impact on purchasing decisions, because there is no sense of "in between" when you are only offered two or three choices.

For example, if most of the putters at the local golf retailer are 35 and 34 inches, many men are naturally going to assume that 34-inch or shorter putters are intended for individuals of diminutive stature. So off they go with a 35-inch putter, not because they've really thought about how it fits their game and physique, but because they've simply made an assumption.

The bottom line is that height is only a factor in establishing putter length, not the sole determinant. Your preferred setup position (more upright vs. more crouched, eyes over the ball vs. inside the target line) and arm length also play a critical role in determining the right putter length.

The good news is that the growing awareness of putter fitting is inspiring more companies to offer a wider variety of lengths. You see more stock 33- and 36-inch models from the big brands today than you did 10 years ago, and custom options are also multiplying among smaller producers.

Lefty's Tall Tale

Among Phil Mickelson's many talents is the apparent ability to make himself taller. Indeed, Mickelson recently claimed to have gained an inch of height through an intensive stretching and fitness regimen, prompting the following headline on Fanhouse.com: "Phil Mickelson Claims to Have Grown an Inch, Will Be Nine Feet Tall by Age 70."

Mickelson reportedly added 1.5 inches to the length of his putter to compensate for his growth spurt. Mickelson's tale is an unusual yet vivid example of how a putter's length should be fitted to the physique and putting approach of the individual, as opposed to the individual trying to fit his or her game to a predetermined putter length.

For example, the SeeMore Putter Company offers custom lengths cut to the half inch from anywhere between 31 and 37 inches, for a total of 13 different putter length options. Similarly, Piretti Fine Putters offers half-inch increments between 32 and 40 inches, for a total of 17 putter length options. Some of the larger brands, such as Never Compromise, are also making it easier to choose custom fitting options.

So, Longer or Shorter?

Pick up your current putter and ask yourself: "Why am I playing with this particular putter length?"

Is it simply because it is the so-called "standard" length? Is it because that's all that was available in your preferred putter model? Is it because someone gave you the putter as a gift, or because you inherited it from a friend or family member?

If so, you may want to step back and experiment with different putter lengths, if only to confirm that what you already have is the right length for you.

> **A Short Story**
>
> Robert Garrigus stands at 5 feet 11 inches, and his career earnings on the PGA Tour are well north of $5 million. The length of his putter? Twenty-eight-and-a-half inches! It just goes to show that there are different strokes for different folks.

It's important to understand that there is nothing inherently wrong or right about 35 inches or 34 inches or any other putter length. It's only when a putter's length is matched to your physique and your game that it becomes wrong or right.

Your putting approach plays a significant role in this equation. For example, many instructors want you to have your eyes directly over the ball—and thus the target line—at setup. Typically, this will result in a more crouched position at setup. Other instructors prefer that your eyes be inside the target line by an inch or two, which will typically necessitate a more upright setup.

These two different approaches necessitate different putter lengths, as they change how close your hands are to the ground. So as you investigate putter lengths, you will also want to have a firm sense of the setup position to which you subscribe.

The bottom line is that putter length plays a role in comfortably achieving *your* preferred setup and putting approach, and the incorrect length can cause nagging performance problems.

When you are in your preferred setup position, the telltale signs of

Hornet's Nest

In recent years, it has become fashionable to recommend putter lengths that are shorter than historical "standards." Indeed, many instructors now say that 35 inches is too long for most male golfers, especially if the goal is to get the eyes directly over the ball.

At the same time, other leading instructors who preach a more upright setup add a word of caution to this trend.

Here is instructor Pat O'Brien's take: "It's hurting a lot of people. It comes down to leverage. If you're forced to bend over more, gravity starts pulling you down toward the ground. And because there's downward pressure being put on the club, it's harder to move. For me, it's all about freedom of motion."

ill-fitting putter length include discomfort and a sense of cramming around the elbows (too long), or a feeling of the arms being too extended and locked (too short).

The flipside is that the incorrect length can actually force you out of your preferred setup position. In an effort to get your arms comfortable with the wrong length, you might find yourself compensating by becoming overly upright or overly crouched. When that happens, your eyes can be too far inside or even outside of the target line, which can cause aiming and alignment issues.

With the right length for your setup, you will make a more fluid and consistent stroke and enjoy the confidence of knowing that your putter length is matched to your putting approach, giving you a proper foundation upon which to practice and improve.

Action Plan

- Do you know the length of your current putter? If not, you should.

- Watch for telltale signs of ill-fitting putter length. For example, if your putter is too long for your preferred setup and putting approach, you might feel some discomfort or a sense of cramming around your elbows. Or if it's too short, you might feel as though your arms are uncomfortably extended or locked, and that your weight is on your toes with gravity pulling you down. In both such cases, the result is excessive tension during the stroke, which can seriously undermine your performance.

🙿 Don't get caught up in comparing yourself to others. For example, if you have longer-than-average arms for your height, you may need to play a shorter putter than your peers of a similar height.

🙿 Be aware that while most major manufacturers offer fairly consistent measurements when it comes to putter lengths, there is some variation in the marketplace. For example, Titleist's Scotty Cameron defines putter length on his web site as follows: "The total length of the putter measured from the butt end of the grip to the sweet spot of the putter. Many manufacturers measure putters differently, measuring from the heel of the putter to the butt of the grip. These putters are usually ½" to 1" longer than Cameron putters."

🙿 Know that a half inch can make a difference in establishing optimal length. It could be that 34.5 or 35.5 inches works best for you.

🙿 If you want to get an approximate sense of how your putter might feel at a shorter length, simply choke down on the grip and stroke some putts.

ʞ If your existing putter proves to be too long, it can easily be shortened by an experienced retailer or fitting professional. The process involves removing the grip, cutting down the shaft and then re-gripping it (often with a brand-new grip, as it can be hard to remove an existing grip without destroying it). Putters can also be lengthened with shaft extenders. It's important to note that changing the length of a putter will also change its swingweight—see the upcoming chapter on putter weight for more information.

4

LIE ANGLE

If you look around your local practice green, it won't be long
before you see someone putting with the putter's toe up in the
air. Sometimes you will see the opposite, with the putter's toe
grounded and its heel raised. Welcome to the world of ill-fitting
lie angles.

Lie angle is the measurement of the angle between the putter's shaft and sole. The easiest way to visualize lie angle is to
think of a typical T-shaped croquet mallet, which naturally has
a lie angle of 90 degrees, as the shaft is perpendicular to the sole.

On a putter, however, the shaft enters the head at a slant, so
you get a smaller figure. Stock putters typically come with a lie
angle between 70 and 72 degrees. A higher number signifies a
more "upright" angle, while a lower number constitutes a "flatter"
lie angle.

When you have the correct lie angle for your setup, the sole
of the putter will be flush with the ground on a level surface. If

a putter's lie angle is too upright for your setup or grip, the putter heel will be grounded and the toe will be lifted. If the angle is too flat, the toe will be grounded and the heel will be lifted. And either scenario can wreak subtle havoc on your putting performance.

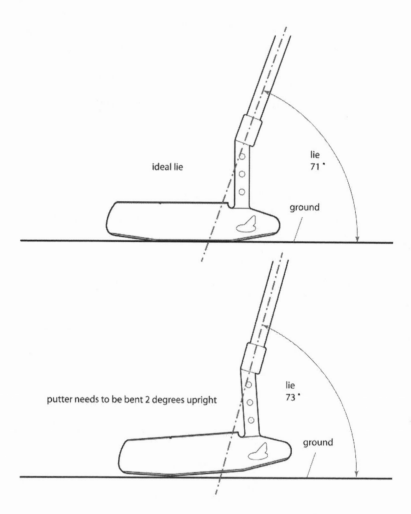

ideal lie

lie
71 °

ground

putter needs to be bent 2 degrees upright

lie
73 °

ground

Find Your Lie

Now, you might ask: As long as the putter face is seemingly square to the target line, why does it matter if the toe is slightly raised?

It matters because of an insidious interaction between the loft of your putter and the lie angle of your putter at contact.

When the lie angle is correct and the sole of your putter is flush to the ground at contact, the loft lifts the ball in a path perpendicular—or square—to the putter face. But when the toe or heel is raised, the presence of loft *changes the plane of the putter face*. With the toe raised, this causes a slight pull to the left. With the heel raised, it causes a push to the right.

As Adam Sheldon, putter designer for Never Compromise and Cleveland Golf, observes, "If you place a stick at 90 degrees to the face of a lofted golf club and then

True Lies

PutterZone.com once asked the crews in a few equipment vans at a PGA Tour event for the most extreme lie angles they've seen on the professional circuits. On the upright side, 78 degrees was cited. On the flat side, 63 degrees was rumored to have been used by one player. That's a spread of 15 degrees. The spread at your local golf retailer, however, is typically around three degrees, with stock lie angles ranging from 70 to 72 degrees.

Also, you might also wonder why you don't see putters with a 90-degree lie angle, essentially like a croquet mallet? That might work for some folks, right? Well, the USGA mandates that putters have a minimum declination angle of 10 degrees, meaning that you can't have a lie angle greater than 80 degrees.

move the club up and down in lie angle, you will see the stick change direction due to the loft."

He adds, "Side spin can be generated when the putter head at impact is not in the correct lie. In other words, if someone putts with the toe in the air, they will generate sidespin at impact and directional control will be affected."

The effect is subtle and often unnoticeable to the golfer, but its impact becomes magnified on longer putts. Many mystifying misses can be traced to an incorrect lie angle.

When the topic of lie angle is being discussed, someone invariably points to the example of some accomplished tour professional who putts with his or her putter's toe in the air.

But the exception doesn't prove the rule, and most professionals are precision-fit for a proper lie angle, because it gives them the best chance to succeed. There are a lot of "don't try this at home" examples on the professional circuits, and just because you see a pro putting with his or her putter's toe in the air does not mean lie angle is unimportant.

Hornet's Nest

An instructional article in a major golf magazine featured a putting tip with the following title: *Accelerate to sink more putts*. The author advised that you "accelerate through impact."

Thirty pages later, in the very same magazine, another article featured the following advice from a leading instructor: "The best strokes reach top speed before impact and maintain that pace through the hitting zone...So thinking 'accelerate through' can hurt you."

We'll let them sort that one out.

Action Plan

❧ Pay attention to lie angle when purchasing a putter. Most manufacturers specify the lie angle of their putters on their web sites.

❧ In your preferred setup, a proper lie angle will result in the sole of your putter being naturally flush with the ground on a level surface.

❧ The way you grip your putter may also change your optimal lie angle. For example, if you switch from gripping the putter along the lifeline of your palm to gripping the putter with the grip running lower along the heel pad of your hand, you will likely need to compensate with a flatter lie angle.

❧ To check the fit of your current putter's lie angle, stand in front of a full length mirror and set up to a ball on a level surface as you normally would (and try not to make any compensations to your setup just because you're now thinking about getting the sole flush to the ground). You will immediately see if the toe or heel is raised. If you don't have a full-length mirror, ask a friend to stand in front of you and report what he or she sees.

🖎 To be really precise, your friend can also insert business cards underneath the heel and toe of the putter in the set-up position. With the correct lie angle, the cards will slide equidistantly underneath either side, confirming that the flat part of the sole is truly flush with the ground. If the heel or toe side is slightly more raised than the other, the card on that side will slide further in than the other.

🖎 If the toe of your putter is raised at setup, your putter is too upright, and you may want to consider a flatter (smaller number) lie angle. For example, if your putter's lie angle is 72 degrees and the toe is raised a few degrees at setup, changing to a lie angle of 70 degrees would solve the issue.

🖎 If the heel of your putter is raised at setup, your putter is too flat, and you may want to consider a more upright (higher number) lie angle.

🖎 Be vigilant about establishing a proper lie angle for your putter. If you dismiss the fact that your putter's heel or toe is raised at setup—and thus upon contact with the ball—you are flirting with trouble in the form of frustrating pulls or pushes.

🖎 A putter's lie angle can typically be adjusted a few degrees in either direction by a qualified professional.

5

LOFT

Like other clubs in your bag, most putters have built-in loft, allowing for the ball to be slightly lifted upon impact. Compared to other clubs, however, the loft on putters is quite slight. The majority of stock putters have a loft ranging between two and four degrees.

The idea behind putter loft is that the ball rests in a natural depression, however slight, when idle on the green. The loft of the putter lifts the ball from this depression upon impact, ideally sending it on a truer roll.

Opinions vary on what constitutes optimal putter loft. As a rule of thumb, however, you need less loft if you play in a dry climate with hard, fast greens, because the natural depression of the ball is shallower on firmer surfaces.

An incorrect loft for your stroke and playing conditions can result in the ball being driven into the ground and bouncing toward the target, or being launched too far and skidding toward the target. The correct loft will promote a true forward roll, minimizing skidding and bouncing for better accuracy and distance control.

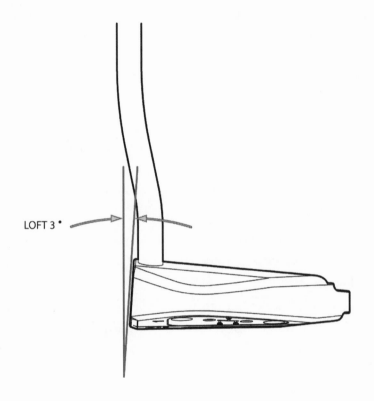

LOFT 3 °

Fixed Loft and Dynamic Loft

The loft of a putter is a fixed physical property of the club, just as it is with your driver, irons and wedges. However, the actual loft of the putter face at impact can be influenced by your mechanics and ball placement. For example, if you tilt the shaft toward the target at impact, then you are essentially de-lofting the putter. Similarly, if you tilt the shaft away from the target at impact, you add loft.

To better understand this phenomenon, consider your 7 iron or any other club in your bag. You can easily change your setup with your 7 iron to send the ball high or to punch it lower, right? On a more subtle scale, the same is true with your putter.

So while the loft of the club may be fixed, what you do with the club can change the actual loft at impact. This actual loft at impact is called "dynamic" loft. Therefore,

A Lofty Lesson

A blurb in Golf Digest noted that Zach Johnson's SeeMore putter has a loft of 3.5 degrees. It further noted, "When he struggles, it's because he creates too much bend in his wrists at the start and adds loft to the putter face. The ball then hops off the face and has a tendency to bounce off line."

This anecdote is a vivid example of fixed loft (the loft of 3.5 degrees built into Johnson's putter) versus dynamic loft (the actual loft of the face at impact), and how stroke mechanics play a major role in the equation.

Of course, most of the time, Johnson's stroke is perfectly matched to his putter's 3.5 degrees of loft, such as when he birded 11 of 16 par 5 holes at Augusta National in 2007 without ever going for the green in two. The result: a green jacket.

if you have a putter with three degrees of fixed loft, but you tilt the shaft two degrees toward the target at impact, you have de-lofted the putter and now have a dynamic loft of one degree. Basic math.

The vertical path of the clubhead at impact is another variable that interacts with putter loft. Vertical path influences launch angle and ultimately shapes how the ball rolls off the face.

But you don't need to get too caught up in the metrics of dynamic loft and vertical path as you search for your optimal putter loft. If you are committed to your putting approach, and if your stroke is fairly consistent, you will have a good baseline for evaluating the fixed loft of a putter.

Good Spin vs. Bad Spin

As with a wedge or any other club, backspin is generated by the putter when the ball is lofted from the ground.

Backspin is wonderful when you hit a wedge shot to the green and want the ball to stick or even roll back toward the hole. But in putting, because the ball travels toward its target along the ground instead of the air, and because you want the ball to go forward not backward, you obviously want to minimize back-spin.

Excessive backspin in putting causes the ball to skid and hop. If the ball is skidding and hopping—particularly along an im-perfect surface such as grass—it is more likely to veer from its original path, and more likely to travel an unpredictable distance.

So topspin is what you want, right? Yes, but not all topspin is created equal. As TaylorMade's chief putting analyst Duane Anderson pointed out to PutterZone.com, you can create topspin by hitting down on the ball and driving it into the turf, but this will also cause the ball to bounce, causing the same problems associated with excessive backspin.

As Duane says, *"You want to get the ball on top of the grass with topspin as efficiently as possible."*

And therein lies the magic that you seek as you investigate different putter lofts. If you consistently see the ball severely skidding or hopping toward the target, something is off in the loft department—either the fixed loft of your putter doesn't fit the playing conditions or it doesn't fit your stroke.

Even with optimal loft, there will be some slight bouncing at the start of the putt before the ball achieves a smooth forward roll. The goal is to shorten this "transition phase" as much as possible.

Hornet's Nest

Some in the industry question the conventional wisdoms of putter loft. For example, Larry Garcia of Q-Roll Golf told PutterZone.com, "You can hardly detect the golf ball indentation on the green that so many manufacturers claim is the reason why the loft is needed, and that is to get the ball out of the indentation. It should be apparent that...lofted face technology is a thing whose time has come and gone."

At the other end of the spectrum you have leading short game instructor Stan Utley, who, in his book *The Art of Putting*, states, "I firmly believe that most players don't have enough loft on their putters."

When the loft is right for your playing conditions and stroke, you will see the ball achieving a quick forward roll, without pronounced wobbling, skidding or bouncing. The ball will seemingly hug the ground, giving it a much better chance of staying on line and reaching its intended mark.

Action Plan

- Don't underestimate the importance of proper loft to putting success. Incorrect loft will work against the goal of achieving quick a forward roll, impacting both directional accuracy and distance control.

- As a general rule, you need more loft for softer playing conditions, and less loft for firmer conditions.

- Understand that the fixed loft of a putter can be manipulated by personal stroke mechanics. Therefore, it's best to be committed to, and consistent with, your stroke before evaluating different putter lofts.

- Some manufacturers claim that their face insert technologies increase launch angle, so that a putter with, say, two degrees of loft will create a higher launch angle than another putter with the two degrees of loft. This is just another reason why you should pay more attention to the actual roll off the face than any preconceived ideas about specific loft measurements.

🖝 When evaluating loft, what you want to see is a short "transition phase," with the ball quickly achieving a clean forward roll. If you sense the ball being pinched against the grass and bouncing excessively, then you likely need more loft. If you see the ball being lifted and skidding excessively, then you likely need less loft.

6

BALANCE

Every putter is balanced in one way or another, and how a putter is balanced can have a significant impact on finding the right fit for your stroke.

The putting stroke falls into two general categories: (1) the inside-to-inside arcing stroke, in which the face of the putter opens and shuts in relation to the target line; and (2) the straight-back-straight-through stroke, in which the face of the putter remains square to the target line during the stroke.

Both types of stroke are preached by leading instructors, and both are seen at the highest levels of golf. Many instructors feel that the straight-back-straight-and-straight-through stroke is unnatural, while others believe that the arcing stroke is too complicated, particularly for amateurs. Also, some instructors preach a hybrid of the two strokes, with the putter arcing on the takeaway, but remaining square to the line through impact.

Regardless, the type of stroke you employ matters because it can determine which type of putter balance is best for your game.

Putter Balancing: Face Balanced and Toe Hang

Like the putting stroke, putter balance falls into two general categories. A "face-balanced" putter will generally appeal to golfers who employ a more straight-back-and-straight-through putting stroke, while a putter with "toe hang," also known as "toe droop," will generally appeal to those with an arcing stroke.

To determine the balance of a putter, simply stick out your hand and place the shaft on an outstretched finger. Find the spot on the lower part of the shaft where you can balance the putter on that finger without assistance from your other hand.

If the face of the putter remains parallel to the ceiling or sky when balanced on your finger, then the putter is face balanced. If the face angles toward the ground, the putter has toe hang, as the toe of the putter is hanging down.

So what determines a putter's balance? When the axis of the shaft (ie: where the shaft points) intersects the head's center of gravity, the putter is naturally face balanced. You see this orientation most often with mallets. However, when the axis of the shaft intersects the rear of the head's center of gravity, as seen on most blades, the putter will have toe hang.

Toe hang comes in varying degrees, depending on the relationship between the shaft axis and the center of gravity. If the toe points straight down at the ground when the putter is balanced on your finger, it's called "toe down" or 6 o'clock, alluding to the hour hand on a clock. If the toe hangs only slightly, you can say that it's at 4 o'clock.

Another way of visually measuring toe hang is to speak of the fractions between face-balanced and fully toe down. In other words, if the toe hangs slightly, you might say the putter has "one quarter toe hang." If it hangs halfway between face-balanced and fully toe down, then you can say it has "half toe hang."

Matching Balance to Stroke

So why do toe-hang putters favor an arcing stroke? Simply put, the sensation of more weight at the toe helps the putter "open and shut" in relation to the target line—essentially a miniature version of the full swing.

Also, the deeper the toe hang—as you go from 4 o'clock to fully toe down at 6 o'clock—the more it will favor a pronounced arc compared to a slighter arc.

Hornet's Nest

Golf Digest ran an article in which the magazine outlined the core teachings of Dave Stockton, Dave Pelz and Stan Utley, which the magazine called the "Big 3" of putting instruction.

In the "Path of The Stroke" section, Stockton's teaching was summed up as "Straight outside or inside going back; along target line going through." Meanwhile, Pelz's preference was summed up as, simply, "straight back and straight through," while Utley's was "on an arc back and through."

So here you have three renowned instructors recommending three different stroke types. It just goes to show that there's more than one way to sink a putt.

Meanwhile, a face-balanced putter will exert less rotational force, making it more favorable to keeping the face square to the target line.

In other words, different putters exert different behavioral properties during the stroke, and finding the right match for *your* stroke can have an impact on your overall performance.

In the midst of re-working his golf swing after his untimely lay-off from the game, Tiger Woods raised eyebrows by switching putters after using the same putter for more than 10 consecutive years. His old putter was an Anser-style blade with toe hang, which he swapped for a fully toe-down putter—indicating that he was matching the balance of his putter to his new stroke patterns.

Woods said, "I have to change everything. It's the whole release pattern…how I release the putter, how I release the short game, how I release irons, drivers, they are all related. You just can't have one swing and not have another; they are all interrelated."

> **Balancing Act**
>
> While most putters are either face balanced or feature some degree of toe hang, there are other balance options on the market. These include "reverse face balanced" putters, with the face parallel to the ground when balanced on your finger; and the "stroke balanced" putter, such as the Odyssey Backstryke and Positive Putter, with the face perpendicular to the ground and facing your target side when balanced on your finger.
>
> Meanwhile, the unconventional Axis1 putter places the center of gravity exactly on the sweet spot of the striking face and in line with the axis of the shaft for "the world's first 100 percent perfectly balanced putter."

He added, "You want to have the same type of swing with the putter all the way up to the driver. It's the same motion just smaller."

On a similar note, leading putting instructor Pat O'Brien told PutterZone.com, "If we stood on the target line as in pool or shuffleboard, then the putter would swing straight back and straight through. But we stand to the side of a golf ball, so physics would say that we have to swing at an arc."

Not everyone, however, believes that the best putting stroke forms a continuous arc. For example, leading instructor Dave Pelz told PutterZone.com, "The rotation of a putter blade through impact does nothing good for a putt, and it does a lot of bad if you hit the ball early or late in your swing, as that means your face will be open or closed…If you're rotating your putter blade, then it's open a lot, open a little, perfect, closed a little bit, and closed a lot. So it's only perfect at one instant in time. I like to extend that time period around impact. I like the putters who bring them square through impact and keep them square."

It's worth noting that while Woods has always played with varying degrees of toe hang in his putter, Pelz prefers a face-balanced putter.

Action Plan

- The balance of a putter can work with—or against—your personal putting stroke. By understanding how your stroke relates to putter balance, you can better determine which putter might best complement and accentuate your game.

- Match the balance of your putter to your stroke. A face-balanced putter favors a straight-back-straight-through stroke. Also, some golfers use an arcing stroke effectively with face-balanced putters. Most mallets are face balanced, as are some blades.

- Meanwhile, a putter with toe hang favors an arcing stroke. Modern blades typically have toe hang at around 4 o'clock or 5 o'clock. A fully "toe-down" putter, often seen in classic blades, favors a more pronounced arc.

- Don't put nostalgia or aesthetics ahead of performance. A lot of golfers play with toe-down classic blades just because they like the looks of them, or because that's what they've always used. But that doesn't mean they have the stroke, or the skill level, to play a toe-down blade with consistency. You want your putter to be pleasing to the eye, but you also want to make sure it's balanced in a way that fits your stroke.

Classic blades are simple and lean,
with the shaft mounted at the heel.

Modern blades come in a variety of shapes and styles, often with the bulk of the head material distributed along the heel and toe.

Mallets also come in a variety of shapes and styles, and exhibit more girth than blades from front to rear.

A **proper lie angle** will result in the sole of the putter being flush with a
level surface at setup and impact, which helps the putt stay on line.

An **ill-fitting lie angle** will result in the heel or toe of the putter raised at setup and impact, which often causes pushes or pulls.

A **face-balanced putter** will remain parallel to the sky or ceiling when balanced on your finger. A face-balanced putter generally favors a straight-back-and-straight-through putting stroke.

A putter with **toe hang** will angle toward the ground when balanced on your finger. A putter with toe hang generally favors an arcing stroke.

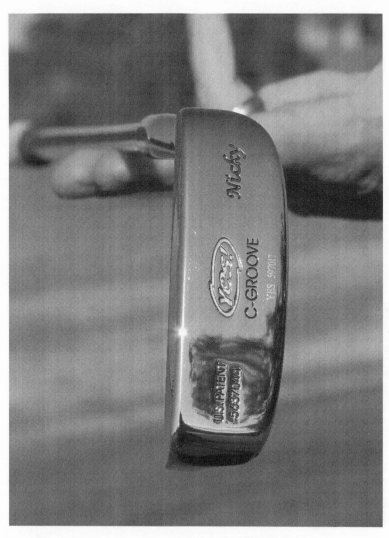

A fully **"toe down" putter** will point straight down toward the ground when balanced on your finger. A toe-down putter generally favors a more pronounced arcing stroke.

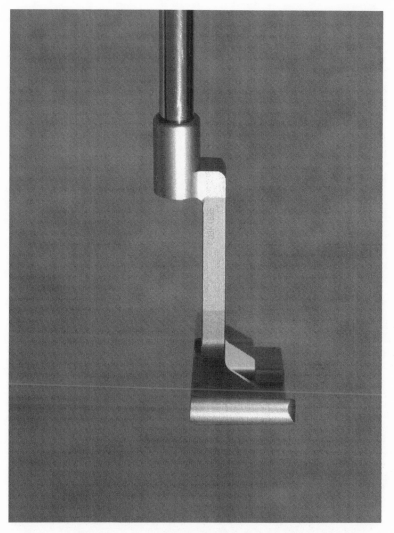

With an **offset putter**, the leading edge of the shaft is forward of the leading edge of the topline. Offset comes in varying degrees, and can shape how the golfer perceives a putter's alignment in relation to the target line.

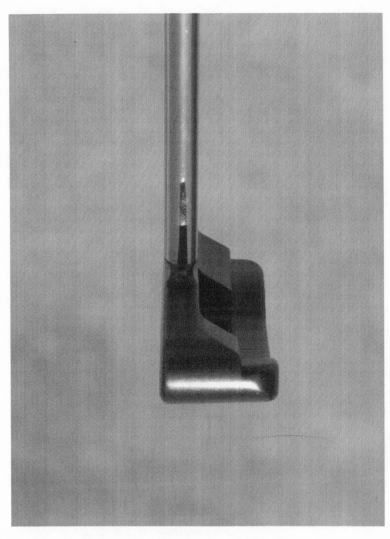

With a **no-offset putter**, the leading edge of the shaft is in direct visual line with the leading edge of the topline.

7

ALIGNMENT

The putting stroke is simply a means to an end. No matter what type of stroke you employ, the goal is to always ensure that the target line is correct, and that the putter face is square to that target line at setup and impact.

For this reason, most putters incorporate visual systems that aspire to aid alignment, from simple sightlines to more elaborate optical technologies.

When the face is square to the correct target line at impact, the ball travels on its intended path. If the face is aiming left or right of the target line at impact, the ball will miss the line accordingly. Needless to say, consistently poor alignment can cause immense frustration around the green.

Maintaining Your Line

Research shows that that alignment is a problem that plagues average golfers. Professionals aren't perfect, but they are better at compensating for it.

Alignment is a difficult concept to capture in words, because it is such an individualized phenomenon. What one golfer "sees" can be quite different that what another golfer sees.

For the purposes of this discussion, we will assume that your target line is correct. In other words, you know where you want the ball to go, you have established a proper target line and you have set yourself up in a manner that is consistent with that line.

At this point, as you address the ball, you need the putter to visually communicate with you and confirm that the face is square to the line.

This is where a lot of golfers fail to pay attention. Take a hard look at what you are seeing. Does the putter face look truly square to the line, or does it appear slightly closed or open? Or is it hard to tell? Are there other alignment features, such as sight-lines, that help verify your line? Or do you see things that confuse your line?

The design of the putter has a huge impact on how you will answer these questions. The angle and offset of the shaft or hosel (see Chapter 11 for more information on offset); the loft and lie angle of the putter; and the shape of the head—all of these things can affect what you perceive, and can either confirm or confuse proper alignment.

For example, a putter with a higher loft will tend to appear more hooked, or closed, than one with lower loft. This optical perception can become even more pronounced on putters with more upright lie angles.

Individual perceptions also play a major role in how a putter appears to be on, or off, target. Eye dominance—everyone is either left or right eye dominant—is often said to be a factor, too.

But whatever the reason, golfers have individual optical tendencies and setup styles that can affect how they "see" the putter at address. So with all other factors being equal, a putter that looks square to the line to one golfer might look hooked or open to another. Therefore, the same putter can convey entirely different alignment experiences to different golfers. Also, just because a putter looks square to the line doesn't mean that it is—there could be other visual factors creating the illusion that the face is square when, in fact, it is slightly open or closed.

The Case for Simplicity

In an interview on PutterZone.com, leading short-game instructor Stan Utley made an interesting observation regarding alignment aids on putters: "I like a putter that's attractive. There are a lot of putters out there that are so complicated when you look down at them. They are meant to help with aiming, but I think they're worse. My buddies with SAM PuttLab did a lot of research on aiming, and the old Acushnet Bullseye was the best-aiming putter. Take that to the bank. The least-complicated putter of all was the easiest one to aim. It didn't even have a line on it."

This is why many fitters use lasers to help determine where you are actually aiming the putter face, as opposed to where you eyes suggest you are aiming it. A laser can cut right to the chase and confirm if a putter is actually aimed where you think it is.

The bottom line is that establishing proper putter alignment can be a tricky and vexing process. But by being aware of the fact that a putter can play tricks on your eyes, you are in a better position to evaluate your own alignment experience.

Once you feel that you have found a putter that gives you the right visual answers, you will want to put it to the test on shorter, level putts, to make sure that what you are seeing is actually what you are getting.

Also, you should not expect any putter alignment system to magically cure alignment issues. You need to do the bulk of the work yourself in lining up your putt and addressing the ball correctly. How-

The Alignment Frontier

Many putter companies have gone to remarkable lengths to help golfers solve their aiming issues. In creating the white Ghost putter, TaylorMade Golf analyzed 25,000 putts and enlisted Indiana University's School of Optometry. To develop its D.A.R.T. putters, Odyssey Golf conducted extensive research into eye-brain relationships, including the Gestalt Effect, which observes the form-generating capability of the senses.

Meanwhile, leading putter fitter David Edel, who is known for his emphasis on alignment, offers a system "of up to 273 million component combinations made up of various putter heads, hosels, offsets, and lie angles to find the combination that corrects for the golfer's natural aim."

ever, alignment systems can accentuate this work and help keep you on the straight and narrow.

Action Plan

🗲 Putter alignment comes into play once you have established the correct target line. The putter should then visually confirm and conform to the line.

🗲 Know that a putter can create optical illusions for a variety of reasons. Not only should the putter face look square to the line—it must actually *be* square to the line. Trial and error can help assure that this is the case. Also, many professional fitters offer technologies that can verify whether or not your putter is aiming where you think it is. Along the way, they can help you find a putter that fits your eyes.

🗲 Test your ability to properly align your putter by stroking numerous shorter, level putts with a direct line to the hole. If you routinely miss to the left or right, you may be experiencing a putter alignment issue. Experiment with other putters to see if something else better fits your eyes and helps you stay square to the target line.

🗲 A putter alignment aid can be a real blessing as long as it fits your eye and sends a calm, confident message.

↙ Make sure that the alignment cues aren't too busy or noisy in a visual sense. If there are too many colors and visual cues jumping out at you, the effect can be distracting or disruptive.

WEIGHT

Putter weight is largely a matter of personal preference, but it can also have a significant impact on how a putter performs in your hands.

The case for a heavier putter is that it can help quiet the small muscles in the hands and wrists for a smoother, more consistent stroke. The case for a lighter putter is that it enables you to take a lighter grip, reducing tension in the stroke.

Golfers who prefer a heavier head typically feel that it stabilizes their stroke, and that it gives them more directional consistency. Golfers who prefer a lighter head often say that it gives them more control and touch.

Putter weight also plays a role in distance control. When a golfer consistently putts the ball too short or too long, the issue can often be traced to a putter weight that is interfering with the ability to achieve optimal stroke speed and overall touch.

Static Weight vs. Swingweight

Before exploring different putter weights, you should understand that putter weight is measured in two ways: (1) the static physical weight of the putter; and (2) the swingweight of the putter. The static weight of a putter is fixed, but the swingweight is fluid, depending on the length and balance point of your putter.

The total static weight of your putter is the combined weight of the grip, shaft and head. Generally speaking, however, the main variable is the weight of the head. When shopping for putters, you will usually see head weight listed as one of the core specifications.

Stock head weights have been trending toward the heavier side in recent years, with most putters now ranging somewhere between 330 and 360 grams.

Meanwhile, the phenomenon of swingweight changes the sensation of static head weight, and it is directly tied to the length of the shaft. For example, if you have a 350-gram head on a 33-inch putter, it will feel lighter than if the same 350-gram head were on a 35-inch putter.

In other words, while static weight is a measurement, swingweight is a sensation or impression. Swingweight has its own measurement system, with monikers such as "D-2" and "D-8," but you do not need to get too caught up in that.

To better understand swingweight, lightly grip your putter or any other club, raise it up in the air and move the head in little circles. The head will feel fairly heavy and wobbly. Now, move your hands down to the middle of the shaft and do the same thing. Your sense of command over the head will change dramatically. The club will feel lighter and easier to control at that shorter length. In other words, the static weight of the head hasn't changed, but the swingweight of the club has been altered.

This is why some putter manufacturers match different head weights to different lengths, in an attempt to maintain a consistent desired swingweight across the board. For example, designer Robert Bettinardi has been known to offer putters in stock weights of 340 grams at 35 inches and 355 grams at 34 inches.

Meanwhile, some manufacturers offer putters with adjustable weighting technology, enabling you to customize the head weight, and thus the swingweight, on the fly.

Most putter manufacturers, however, don't account for swingweight differences, using the same

Heavy Metal

While putter head weights have been trending upward in recent years, one putter blew the doors wide open: the Heavy Putter by Boccieri Golf.

On paper, a 400-gram head seems like it would create an out-of-control swingweight. But the head weight is only part of the Heavy Putter story. The other part is a counterweight embedded in the grip end of the shaft, which raises the balance point and makes the heavy head easy to control.

According to creator Stephen Boccieri, "The Heavy Putter's greater total weight engages the golfer's larger and more stable muscles, while the higher balance point disengages the golfer's hands, promoting a smoother, more consistent stroke."

head weight for a 34-inch putter as they do for a 35-inch putter. That doesn't mean there is something wrong with one or the other, but it does mean that these two putters will feel slightly differently in terms of their weighting.

Adding a heavy oversized grip to a putter can also noticeably change swingweight. Without getting too technical, adding weight to the grip end of the shaft raises the balance point of the club. Just as adding weight to the head lowers the balance point and naturally makes the club feel heavier, adding weight to the grip end of the club will make it feel lighter.

Action Plan

- Putter weight is largely a matter of personal preference, but if you are experiencing issues with distance control or keeping the putter on line through the stroke, you may want to consider experimenting with different head weights.

- Understand that a putter's head weight is not the sole determinant of how heavy or light a putter feels. Due to the phenomenon of swingweight, with all other things being equal, a 350-gram head will feel lighter on a shorter shaft than on a longer shaft.

- Be aware that while most manufacturers use the same head weight at different lengths on a given putter model, others offer different head weights for different lengths. You will therefore want to do your homework before purchasing a putter and make sure that you are getting the weight (and swingweight) you want.

☞ The phenomenon of swingweight is added reason why you should establish your correct putter length before purchasing a putter. Yes, you can later shorten or lengthen your putter, but this will change the swingweight and thus your relationship to that putter.

☞ Adding a heavier grip will raise the balance point of the putter and can noticeably alter the swingweight, making the putter feel lighter. Keep this in mind if you are considering installing an oversized grip on your putter.

FEEL

Feel is a lot of things, and it means different things to different people. As Stan Utley writes in *The Art of Putting*, "(Feel is) one of those things that's really hard to describe, but you know it when you 'feel' it."

Feel is probably best described as a combination of audio and tactile feedback—the merging of sound and touch into a single impression.

Feel should not be underestimated as a component of your overall fitting efforts. It may not be as easy to measure or quantify as putter length or lie angle, but it is no less important to cultivating a rewarding putting experience.

Sound and Touch

Oh, What A Feeling

In an article about the almost extrasensory abilities of certain top professionals, Michael Bamberger of Sports Illustrated wrote about how Brad Faxon was once having a custom putter made for him and was unsatisfied until a "sound slot" was cut into the sole (a sound slot is a narrow slit along the flange of the putter).

Observed Bamberger, "What did that little slot, too narrow to fit a resort scorecard, give Faxon? The sound he wanted, the swingweight he wanted, the coefficient of restitution (COR) he wanted. How much less did the putter weigh with the slit cut into it? It lightened the head by the weight of two dimes, if that. But these are not ordinary people with standard-issue senses."

The feel of a putter is determined by a variety of factors, including the type of metal used in the head, the shape and acoustics of the head, and even the grip and shaft. A face insert or face grooves can also shape the feel of a putter, and the type of ball you use will also impact the feel off the face.

It's easy to overlook the role of sound as a component of feel, but a lot of what you think you are feeling in a tactile sense is actually what you are hearing, just as the aroma of a wine or food largely determines what you taste.

Phil Mickelson once swapped out the insert in his Odyssey putter for the sake of audio feedback. He had changed to a softer ball, which he said wasn't making enough sound at impact. As he told Golf Digest: "I switched back to a harder insert to get back that sound I like...It's impossible to overstate how important sound is to your feel on the green."

As with music, however, the sound that Phil Mickelson likes might be quite different from what you or Tiger Woods likes. Sound is important yet also very personal. Only you will know what sounds best to you.

Like sound, your tactile preferences are also very personal. Some golfers prefer a soft or springy putter, others prefer a clicky or firm sensation upon impact.

What you want to look for is a sensation that you find rewarding when you hit the sweet spot. Does it hit just the right "note" in your hands? Does it make you want to keep putting, to keep seeking that reward? If so, then you are on to something.

Feedback

Feel, however, is not just a sensual preference. It is the foundation of feedback, or the way in which the putter communicates what it is doing or what it has done.

Over time, the feedback of a putter can shape and elevate your performance, because it informs you about your putting. When you miss or make a putt, or when your distance control

Humble Heroes

While pricey Scotty Cameron putters are a favorite on the PGA Tour, plenty of professionals wield humble sticks, too.

Consider Jerry Kelly, who purchased a $69 Cleveland Classic putter off the rack and promptly racked up a $1 million victory.

Or how about Jim Furyk, who plucked an old Yes Sophia putter out of a used putter bin for $39 and promptly used it to claim the $1.35 million winner's prize at the Tour Championship and the $10 million bonus as the winner of the 2010 FedEx Cup playoffs.

is good or bad, the feedback from your putter can register on a biomechanical level, adding to your overall sense of what just happened.

When it comes to feedback, some putters feel more uniform and quiet across the face, while others are very nuanced, vividly communicating the slightest miss-hit to the hands and ears.

If you are obsessive about precision and detail, you may want to consider a putter that is "talkative" in its feedback. If you prefer to be more loose and free-spirited when it comes to putting, then you may want your putter to be a little less of a nag.

As a general rule, however, you will want to choose a putter that sounds consistent with its touch. If the putter feels firm in a tactile sense yet soft in an audio sense, or vice versa, you may have a difficult time reconciling the overall feedback.

At the end of the day, the right feel will encourage you to fall in love with your putter, and to develop a lasting relationship with it. You may even be inspired to practice more, too. Along the way, you will develop familiarity, which will then breed confidence, which can ultimately be the difference between a two-putt and a three-putt.

Action Plan

🦶 You spend more time with your putter than any other club in an average round of golf. It's the most intimate club in your bag. Therefore, you should really love your putter, which is impossible to do if you hate the way it feels.

🦶 Understand that the type of ball you use will shape the feel, and thus the feedback, of a putter. When testing putters for feel, test them with the type of ball you typically use (see the Tips & Tricks chapter for more on this subject).

🦶 There is no right feel in general, just a right feel for *you*. The important thing is to not get so dazzled by a putter's looks or marketing hype that you overlook the importance of feel when purchasing a putter.

🦶 Are you listening to your putter? The audio and tactile qualities of your putter at impact can provide valuable feedback.

10

GRIP

The size and style of a putter's grip can have a significant impact on fit and performance, but you wouldn't know it by looking around your average golf retail outlet.

Indeed, stock putters typically come with only one preinstalled grip size. Some come with thin grips, others come with fatter grips. You get what you get, regardless of how big or small your hands are. Therefore, when it comes to purchasing a putter, most people don't give the size of the grip any thought, largely because they are unaware that other options might be available.

Compare this to tennis racquets, which are routinely offered with different grip sizes at the point of retail purchase to ensure a proper fit with a wide variety of hand sizes. The golf industry has a long way to go on this front.

That said, more and more of the smaller putter companies now offer multiple grip size and style options at the point of purchase, particularly when selling direct to the consumer. Some of the bigger brands also now offer different grip options, but typically only on custom orders.

Also, the choices in aftermarket grips are growing, enabling you to replace the stock grip with one that better fits your hands.

Get A Grip

Timber!

So what's that tree trunk-looking thing on the end of PGA Tour professional K.J. Choi's putter? It's the Super-Stroke, a distinctively oversized taper-free grip that aims to relax the hands, inhibit wrist breakdown and engage the shoulders for a smoother, more consistent putting stroke. While the SuperStroke grip looks like it would add a lot of weight to the top of the putter, the latest models are surprisingly light, which minimizes the oversized grip's impact on the club's swingweight.

In the words of Golf Pride, a leading grip manufacturer, "Putter grips are the most touched, most used, and most overlooked piece of equipment in the bag. Because putter grips are used once, twice, and unfortunately sometimes three or four times per green, they deserve far more attention and care than they typically get."

But as with many aspects of putters and putting, the expert opinion on optimal grip size is divided, signaling that it ultimately comes down, once again, to finding the right balance between personal preference and performance.

Those who recommend a thinner grip say that it maintains a better sense of feel and touch. Those who recommend a fatter grip say that it quiets the small muscles and helps prevent wrist breakdown in the stroke.

These recommendations are, of course, dependent on the size of your hand—what seems thin to someone with large hands will feel larger to someone with small hands.

Two other factors in finding the right grip are shape and tactile quality. Putter grips generally fall into two shape categories, the paddle grip and the pistol grip. The paddle grip is flat along the front, while a pistol grip is flat along the front with a widened arch along the back.

Tactile quality also varies from grip to grip. Some grips feel more tacky than others. Some are soft and supple in the hands, others are firmer. Your choice in tactile quality will come down to what you find most comfortable.

What you ultimately need to know is that the size of the grip, and how it feels in your hands, can shape your putting performance and make a difference in your score.

Broken Arrow

When Kenny Perry enjoyed a resurgence on the PGA Tour a few years ago, he gave a lot of credit to his putter, a PING G2i Craz-E model. It was a hand-me-down from a member at his golf club in Vero Beach. "I've putted beautifully ever since he gave me this putter," Perry said.

But then disaster struck, and the tip of the shaft on Perry's beloved putter broke. Perry promptly put a backup Craz-E putter into play, but, he said, "That putter didn't look or feel the same." So the broken club was overnighted from the tournament in Hawaii to PING's headquarters in Phoenix for an emergency repair.

Apparently, finding just the right putter for you and your game can make a big difference. Just ask Kenny Perry.

Action Plan

⚑ Don't assume that the grip that came pre-installed on your putter is the right fit for your hands. Numerous aftermarket grips are available in a wide variety of sizes and shapes, and you need to be aware that there could be a better fit out there.

⚑ A qualified retailer or club fitter can easily change your putter grip for a nominal cost. The process involves removing the existing grip, either by blowing it off with an air compressor, or, if necessary, cutting it off. After the shaft is cleaned, double-sided tape and solvent are applied to the shaft, and the new grip is slipped into place.

⚑ If your stroke is wristy and routinely breaks down through impact, it could be a sign that your putter grip is too thin for your hands.

⚑ If you feel regular tension in the fingers and hands, or if it seems that you are lacking sufficient touch in your putting stroke, you may want to consider a thinner grip.

⚑ If you are at your wit's end, you can try an oversized grip that is designed to override the small muscles and take the wrists entirely out of the equation. What you sacrifice in touch you might gain in stability.

⟆ If your replacement grip is larger and heavier than the original, know that it may noticeably alter the swingweight of your putter (see the Weight chapter for more information on swingweight).

⟆ Don't underestimate the impact of comfort in your putter grip. An uncomfortable grip can create an unsettling sensation as you're standing over your putt. It can also cause undue hand fatigue when you are practicing your putting.

11

PUTTER ATTRIBUTES & TECHNOLOGIES

When shopping for a putter, you will encounter a dizzying array of specifications and technological buzzwords. We have already covered the core fitting specifications, such as length, loft and lie angle. Following are overviews of additional putter attributes and buzzwords that you will want to understand and navigate as you shop for a putter.

Shaft Placement and Offset

Shaft style and placement varies from putter to putter. A putter shaft can be straight or curved as it approaches the putter head. A shaft can also be mounted into a "hosel," a joint that extends from the putter head. Hence, you will often see terms such as "double-bend shaft" or "crank-neck hosel" when perusing different putters. Also, a shaft can be mounted in the heel or center of the putter head, as well as in between, so you will see terms such as "heel shafted" and "center shafted."

Meanwhile, depending on how the shaft curves and/or how the hosel is constructed, a putter can have varying degrees of "offset."

In a putter with no offset, the leading edge of the shaft is in direct visual line with the leading edge of the putter's topline at setup. You typically see this with straight shafts that have no bend as they enter the head. You also occasionally see putters with "onset," whereby the leading edge of the shaft is slightly behind the leading edge of the putter's topline.

In a putter *with* offset, the leading edge of the shaft is visually forward of the leading edge of putter's topline at setup. The term "full-shaft offset" means that the degree of offset is equal to the width of the shaft, while "half-shaft offset" signifies that the offset is roughly equal to half of the width of the shaft.

Offset putters are preferred by golfers who like to have their hands slightly ahead of the ball during the putting stroke. Some also believe that eye dominance plays a role in determining the optimal amount of offset for the golfer.

Putter Metals

While some putters are made from wood or advanced plastics, most are made from a variety of metals. The original PING putters were made of manganese bronze. Brass, titanium, aluminum and copper are also used in the manufacturing of putters.

However, steel is the metal that dominates the putter category today, and most high-end putters come in stainless steel or carbon steel.

Stainless steels tagged by the monikers of 303 or 304 are popular for their quality and relative softness. Carbon steel is naturally even softer, but it requires more maintenance for guarding against rust if it is not coated or plated.

Some golfers gravitate toward carbon steel for its softer feel. That said, the feel of a putter is also determined by the shape, construction and plating (if any) of the head. This is why some stainless steel putters can feel softer than certain carbon steel putters.

Milled Putters

When shopping for a putter, you will often encounter the word "milled," and you will notice that the term is most often associated with higher prices.

Most putters are produced by one of two processes: casting or milling. Milling is considered to be a superior method to casting, and milled putters are therefore prized for having a superior feel to cast putters.

Casting is the process of pouring molten metal into molds, after which the metal cools and the molds are removed. Milling, on the other hand, is a machining process that essentially cuts and sculpts the putter from a solid block of metal with remarkable precision and reliability.

Naturally, milling is more costly than casting, hence the heftier price tags on milled putters. The base metal for milling is more expensive, but it offers superior grain and quality.

Famed putter maker T.P. Mills is largely credited with popularizing the milled putter in the 1960s with his hand-milled flatsticks. Putter design pioneer Dick DeLaCruz took putter milling to the broad market in the 1980s with the first CNC milled putter, the Callaway Bobby Jones hickory-shafted blade. CNC (for computer numerical controlled) machines are still used today.

If you seek a truly milled putter, look for the term "100-percent milled." Some putters are initially cast, with the surfaces subsequently milled to ensure precision flatness. This type of "skim milling" is a nice touch on many putters, but it doesn't qualify as 100-percent milled.

Prior to milling, putters may also be forged, whereby the metal is hammered and ground into its initial shape. Forging is said to improve the consistency of the metal for improved feel.

Face Inserts

Face inserts are inserts that are mounted into the face of the putter, and which are of a different material than the rest of the putter head.

The intent behind face inserts is to impart a feel that is different, and ideally more appealing, than simple steel. Inserts often feel softer than steel, but not always. Inserts may also be designed to impart different rebound, launch angle and distance-control properties. Some inserts are also made of low-density materials, which can help redistribute weight to increase moment of inertia (or MOI, which is explained below).

Face insert materials are varied, from copper to elastomer, aluminum to urethane. As with so many things in putting, face inserts come down to personal preference. Some golfers prefer the familiarity of steel, while others embrace the unique qualities of certain inserts.

Face Grooves

Putter face grooves are grooved patterns on the face of a putter designed to grip or otherwise engage the ball in a manner that promotes quicker topspin for a truer roll. Grooves can also affect feel and ball speed by limiting the surface area in contact with the ball.

The topic of face grooves is a bit of a hornet's nest in the putter industry. Some swear by them while others remain skeptical. Clouding the discussion is the fact that grooved putters often have lower stock lofts, prompting some to suggest that this lower loft is what generates quicker topspin on testing surfaces that are harder than the average green.

What's important to know is that grooves might help, and that they likely don't hurt. When testing putters with grooves, keep a close eye on the roll, and if you like what you see, it might be a good fit for you. And remember that your putter's loft at impact influences the quality of the roll as well.

Moment of Inertia (MOI)

Moment of Inertia (MOI) is the poster child of putter buzz-words that are frequently used by manufacturers but rarely explained to the average golfer.

MOI is a measurement of a putter head's weight properties. A putter with high MOI is more resistant to twisting and turning upon impact. Consequently, if you errantly strike the ball away from the center of the putter face—say, toward the toe—a putter with high MOI will better resist twisting off target. Thus, higher MOI generates enhanced forgiveness and accuracy on miss-hits.

MOI is increased when weight is moved away from the putter head's center of gravity during the design process. The pursuit of extra-high MOI often results in unique putter shapes.

MOI should probably not be your first concern when purchasing a putter. If a putter fits your game and feels great, *and* it has high MOI, then that's great. However, fit and feel should be your priority, because the better the fit and feel, the fewer miss-hits you will have in the first place.

Heel-Toe Weighting

The term "heel-toe weighting" refers to putters with the bulk of their head weight distributed along the heel and toe. The classic PING Anser is heel-toe weighted, with a cavity behind the center of the face, and with the mass of the head placed along the heel and toe.

You sometimes hear the term "heel-toe balanced," but there really isn't such a thing—it's just an unfortunate catchphrase. As detailed in an earlier chapter, there are two general categories of putter balance: face balanced and toe hang. The same heel-toe weighted putter head can fall into either category, depending on where the axis of the shaft lies in relation to the head's center of gravity. Heel-toe weighting is a design characteristic, not a balancing characteristic.

So what does heel-toe weighting achieve? It elevates the MOI by distributing more weight to the perimeters of the putter head.

Belly Putters and Long Putters

Belly putters (longer putters designed to anchor against the stomach when putting) and long putters (even longer than belly putters, often anchored to the chest) are always an option.

Several accomplished PGA Tour professionals use these putters, but typically only after they have become frustrated and exhausted with traditional putters. That said, long putter usage is growing on the professional circuits, bringing them more into the mainstream. Your choices in putters (and putting instruction) are much more numerous when you use a traditional-length putter. However, belly and long putters may be worth exploring if you are at your wit's end with traditional putters.

A Note on Technologies

Don't let the vast array of technological choices overwhelm you. There is no single putter that "has it all." Instead, think of areas of your game that need help, and begin by finding a putter that will address those areas.

For example, if you have ongoing issues with alignment, then start by investigating some of the putters known for their alignment aids. Or if you are struggling with finding the right putter weight, then consider putters with adjustable weighting technologies that will give you flexibility going forward. If you are having trouble imparting consistent roll, then try out some groove-faced putters, or experiment with different lofts.

Lastly, never overlook the importance of putter feel. If you don't love the feel of your putter—no matter how tricked out it is—you won't love putting with it. So make sure that feel doesn't get lost in the technological shuffle.

12

"PUTTING" IT ALL TOGETHER

Are you pumped up? Good. You should be. You understand how a putter works, and what to look for when it comes to finding the right fit for your game. You are now ready to put it all together.

This book is presented in a spirit of simplicity. You should be inspired, not intimidated, by your newfound awareness of putter fitting fundamentals. Don't worry if you can't absorb every last detail before buying a putter. The point isn't to make your purchasing decision more complicated, but rather to simply cut through the jargon and demystify the critical factors in finding the right putter for you and your game.

If it seems overwhelming at first, break it all down into parts, and take a simple step-by-step approach: Find the putter length that fits your setup and fosters a fluid stroke. Make sure that the lie angle is correct, so that the sole is flush with the ground at setup and impact. Calibrate your loft so that the ball achieves quick forward roll off the face. Match the balance of the putter to your stroke so that it flows naturally. Verify that the putter's alignment features confirm, rather than confuse, the target line. Establish a putter weight and grip size that enable you to putt with both control and comfort.

Each of these steps will take you further along the path to the destination of putter perfection. It may take some time, but it will be worth the effort. Along the way, you will ultimately raise your game and lower your scores.

TIPS & TRICKS

Following are some tips and tricks to help guide you through the putter purchasing process and to brighten your life around the green.

Get on The Ball

Golf balls come in varying degrees of surface and auditory properties, which can greatly impact the feel and feedback of a given putter. Therefore, you should always bring your own preferred golf balls to the store when trying out putters.

If you rely on a random assortment of golf balls (ie: those provided by the store) to evaluate putters, you really don't have a baseline for your evaluations, and you may be disappointed when you take a putter home only to find out that its feel and feedback behave differently with your own preferred golf balls. A putter that felt soft and supple in the store might suddenly feel firm or hard, or vice versa.

So get on the ball by packing your own when shopping for a putter.

Know Your Rights

Online shopping puts the entire world of putters at your fingertips, making it easier than ever before to find the right putter. No longer are you confined to what's in stock at your local retailer.

One downside to buying online, however, is that you can only sample the putter after you have purchased it. For this reason, you will want to carefully review the refund and return policies of the online merchant who is selling you the putter. Some are more lenient than others.

Does the wrapping still need to be on the grip when you return it? How about the head? If the wrapping still needs to be on the head, that's a red flag. It means that, sure, they offer a full refund— as long as you never putt a ball with it. Even if you are allowed to unwrap the putter, you should probably confine your testing to a non-abrasive surface (such as your carpet) to ensure that you don't scratch the putter and ruin your chances for a return.

When in doubt, call to speak with someone and confirm the return policy, and take a note of whom you spoke with, and when you spoke with them, just in case.

Some of the smaller putter companies allow you to buy putters direct, and they are usually very good about making sure you are happy with your putter. Still, you will want to call to make sure you understand their policies.

Buyer Beware

Did you know that golf club counterfeiting is a serious problem? For example, not long ago, federal authorities apprehended two individuals accused of operating a major golf equipment counterfeiting operation based in North Carolina.

The counterfeit brand name products were being imported from Asia and sold on eBay. Thousands of fake golf products were seized, including counterfeit products bearing the trademarks of Titleist, Cobra, Scotty Cameron, Cleveland, Nike, PING, Callaway and TaylorMade. Major raids have also been conducted at golf equipment counterfeiting facilities in China and elsewhere.

You can certainly find some great putter deals on eBay and other online outlets. However, you will want to be careful and buy only from reputable sellers.

Skip The Socks

Indoor putting practice is not only fun, it's often essential to keeping your game sharp, particularly in regions where the winters are long and harsh. A short carpet is all you really need if you're just trying to groove your stroke. But there are numerous aids that can help as well, from putting gates to indoor cups, putting mats to more expensive indoor putting greens.

One mistake that golfers often make when putting indoors is not wearing proper footwear. Now, of course you don't want to walk around the house in your golf spikes. But neither do you want to practice your putting in your socks or in low slippers.

Why? Because such footwear doesn't mimic the height of your golf shoes. In your socks, you might be a half inch to an inch shorter than when you are wearing your golf shoes. So when you practice in your socks, it's like adding a half inch or inch to your putter length, which changes the putter's fit. And if you have to ask why that matters, then you need to re-read this book!

So when practicing indoors, it's best to wear a pair of shoes that is the same, or close to, the height as your golf shoes. This will enable you to practice with the same fit and stroke that you will take to the green. And if you're lounging around in your socks and can't resist taking a few strokes with your putter, at least choke down a bit on the grip to compensate for your missing shoes.

Cover Up

A word to the wise: Use a putter cover! Not only will it save your putter, it might save your wedge, too.

It's amazing to see how many golfers are so careful to cover their driver while leaving their putters exposed to "bag chatter," the nicking and denting that occurs as clubs rattle around in the golf bag.

Putting is a game of inches, half inches and, at times, centimeters. For this reason, putter designers go to great technological lengths to create milling patterns, grooves or inserts that deliver consistent impact as precisely and reliably as possible.

In other words, a nick in the putter face can undo a lot of hard work—and it could conceivably knock your putts off line, too.

A putter cover comes in handy around the green, too. How many of us have pulled a wedge and a putter out of the bag to finish a hole, only to drive or walk off with the wedge forgotten on the fringe? At best, it's inconvenient to retrieve the wedge. At worst, the wedge vanishes into the bag of a thief.

But if you are in the habit of using a putter cover, you can leave it on until you're ready to putt. And when you are ready to putt, you can habitually toss the cover next to your wedge. And guess what? After putting, your first impulse will be to re-cover your putter, compelling you to retrieve your putter cover—and making it nearly impossible to forget the wedge lying next to it.

The bottom line is that if you leave your putter uncovered, bad things can happen. This game is hard enough as it is, so do yourself a favor and cover up your putter.

Invest in Love

The putter is not only the most important club in the bag, it's also the most personal and most intimate club. You should really love your putter, because you'll be spending a lot of time with it.

Therefore, it may be worth paying extra for a putter that you love to hold and behold, and that just feels right. Such a putter will inspire you to practice more often, which will ultimately help you sink more putts when it counts.

Some people contend that $200 or $300 is a ridiculous price to pay for a putter when there are cheaper sticks that roll the ball just fine. Yet no one seems offended by golfers paying $400 for the latest mass-produced driver, even though the putter is used nearly three times as often as the driver in an average round of golf. In that context, it is quite reasonable to invest in a high-quality putter that may cost $200 or more.

So if you're smitten with a particular putter but unsure of the price, you may want to just go ahead and splurge, even it means waiting to save up or looking under the couch cushions for loose change. In the long run, your investment will likely pay off.

SPECIAL THANKS

In writing *Putter Perfection*, I sought the input of expert technical advisors in the fields of putting instruction and putter design. They graciously lent their time and expertise, and ultimately made this a better book. They are:

Pat O'Brien

Pat O'Brien is the putting instructor to major champions Zach Johnson and Stewart Cink and many other PGA Tour professionals. He is also the teaching professional at Lakewood Country Club in Dallas, Texas, and the global ambassador for the SeeMore Putter Company. He can be reached through his website at www.patobriengolf.com.

Adam Sheldon

Adam Sheldon is the master craftsman for Never Compromise putters, and he also oversees the engineering and design of Cleveland Golf putters. He joined Cleveland Golf in 2001 and wields 10 years of experience in designing putters. His recent successes include the Cleveland Classic and Never Compromise Gambler Limited putter lines. Visit www.nevercompromise.com for more information.

ACKNOWLEDGEMENTS

Thanks to my wonderful wife Malei and my son Easton, who so generously tolerate my time on the putting green (and behind the computer screen); to my friends at GolflandWarehouse.com, the biggest little golf retailer on the web, for their generous support and enthusiasm; to Josh Babbitt of The Hacker's Paradise, for his good cheer and great advice; and to everyone in the golf industry who shares their ideas, thoughts, news and products with PutterZone.com.

Visit us online for the latest putter news and reviews, and join our mailing list for exclusive updates, contests and more.

www.PutterPerfection.com

www.PutterZone.com

Save 10%
on your next new putter purchase!*

go to:

GOLFLANDWAREHOUSE.COM

Use referral code:
putterzone
at checkout!

www.golflandwarehouse.com

Made in the USA
Lexington, KY
21 September 2012